Seraphim of Sarov

front cover illustration for the original 1913 Russian edition of Святой Серафим *("Saint Seraphim"),* by Margarita Woloshin

Seraphim of Sarov

A Russian Saint's Story

Margarita Sabashnikova Woloschin

translated by Irina Segal

SteinerBooks
2025

Copyright © 2025 by SteinerBooks

SteinerBooks | Anthroposophic Press
834 Main Street, P.O. Box 358
Spencertown, New York 12165
steinerbooks.org

Original translation from the Russian language by Irina Segal.

ISBN: 978-1-62148-390-8
eBook ISBN: 978-1-62148-391-5

All rights reserved. No part of this book may be reproduced in any form withoutwritten permission from the publisher, except for brief quotations embodied incritical articles for review.

Preface

Margarita Woloschin's narrative of the life of Seraphim of Sarov, translated into English here for the first time, was published in Moscow in 1913, just ten years after Sarov's canonization by the Russian Orthodox Church in July of 1903.

Seraphim's life has attracted the interest of philosophers, theologians, religious leaders (Pope John Paul II), writers, and poets. At the beginning of the twentieth century, neo-Orthodox thinkers like Bulgakov, Florensky, Rozanov, and Berdyaev, and writers of the Silver Age, Bely and Merezhkovsky, turned their attention to the life of elder Seraphim.

"Elder" (*starets*) is not an appointment in the Church which can be made and filled, nor is it an order in the hierarchy which can be conferred in ordination. It expresses a spiritual authority which arises from the inner life of the elder himself; it can be revealed and recognized but not claimed or given. The monk whose spiritual powers are manifested, retains his own character, transfigured or sublimated and informed by a higher power. Elder Seraphim was one such vital personality combining and fusing in himself many facets of religious enlightenment. The touch of the healer, the insight of the seer, the eccentricity of the Fool in Christ, the glow of the mystic—all these can be seen in him. Saint Seraphim's life and deeds were felt to contain a new and profound revelation centering on the Holy Spirit.

By 1912, Woloschin was one of a small group of young Russians, which included the writer Andrei Bely and the painter Aasya Turgineff,† who had taken a keen interest in the writings and lecturing activity of Rudolf Steiner, attending his lecture cycles throughout Europe whenever possible, and, once construction began, living and working near Dornach, at the site of the first Goetheanum building.

In her memoir, *The Green Snake*,‡ Woloschin describes how

> in 1912, a group of Russian Old Believers petitioned to the Moscow publishing house *Dukhovnoye Znanie*, expressing a desire to receive a book about the holy elder Seraphim, free from the unctuousness inherent in ordinary Orthodox Synod publications. The publisher gave this order to me. In my next conversation with Rudolf Steiner, I asked him about this personality, so significant for Russia, whose presence in the people's consciousness was still vividly felt. Saint Seraphim died in 1833. You could still meet people who knew him.

---

† See *Reminiscences of Rudolf Steiner* by Andrei Belyi; Aasya Turgenieff, and Margarita Voloshin (Adonis Press, 1987).

‡ *The Green Snake: An Autobiography* (Floris Books, 2010)

The stories about his words and deeds, especially about the healings that also took place after his death until our time, were not fiction. I can say that his image overshadowed the Russia of my time.

Rudolf Steiner knew everything about him and said: "Saint Seraphim is one of the greatest individuals. But in this incarnation, he did not act through thought. You need to peer into his deeds. Go to where he lived, then you will feel how to write about him."

This she did, traveling back to Russia and spending the next months following the traces of the beloved Saint while composing the text that follows. She arrived at his monastery just before the Saint's birthday:

So, my father and I went to the Sarov Monastery, located among the vast forests of the Tambov province. It was on the eve of St. Seraphim's birthday, celebrated on July 19. After a rather long journey by rail, we got off at the station, from where we had to ride horses for several more hours. Although it was harvest time, thousands and thousands of pilgrims went to the monastery for the feast.

...In Russia in those days, the sick in the villages were almost completely deprived of medical care. Hospitals and outpatient clinics, located at a great distance from each other, were often in disrepair, without medicines. Doctors, out of desperation, became drunkards. The sick and their loved ones bore their God-sent destiny with patience and humility. In these people: crippled, seriously ill, consumptive, tormented by suffering, but not losing their uprightness in this suffering, without bitterness, a great secret was felt. Here the life of nature gives way to the spirit. It shines into our world as if through a window. It looks at us through the soul, crucified in life.

...The fiery will of Seraphim absorbed so deeply the forces of the creative Word that his own life forces merged with the pure, holy and healing cosmic forces active in nature. The rock on which he prayed, the spring he blessed, belonged to his own being, for his spirit united with the spirit of the Earth, which, after Golgotha became the body of Christ. That rock towers in the worlds where Seraphim's will operates; and that spring, gushing from the earth, flows with love, as from Seraphim's own heart, with love that mends human destinies and heals human flesh.

Compositionally, the story follows a traditional form of hagiography, with detailed descriptions of Saint Seraphim's biography that are told in simple yet pictorial language and are accompanied by Woloschin's commentaries and reflections. Presenting the most remarkable facts and key stages of Saint Seraphim's life, Woloshin's storytelling contemplates deeply about the nature of miracles, the Holy Spirit, the human soul and spirituality, the Word of God, and silence.

Woloshin's telling of the story of Saint Seraphim's remarkable life, informed as it is, quite naturally, by both the Russian Church and anthroposophy, is a remarkably fresh testament to the beauty and power of human love and sacrifice, in service of Christ.

The warmth of heart and love of Seraphim, evident both in and between the lines of this story, are both awesome and humbling. At least one person, in reading it, felt that her soul grew warmer, as she began to pray from the heart, from her feeling human nature. And just as the air rises when it gets warm, so the soul can ascend to where the true self resides.

Saint Seraphim of Sarov

Saint Seraphim of Sarov
Unknown illustrator, from the 1913 Russian edition.

Holy Elder Seraphim... From the pine thicket of the forest, he walks: bent, leaning on an axe, wearing a rumpled skullcap, a white robe, large copper cross on his chest, a bag over his shoulders with a book of the Gospels in it.

White as snow are his hair and beard, his cheeks sunken, nose pointy and short. Almond shaped blue eyes stare intently from under long eyebrows. The intensity of those eyes is extraordinary.

All the power of a deep sorrow lives in them, a sorrow that knows the stern unrelenting truth about the world, a truth that burns like an open wound. All the strength of a flaming absolute joy lives in those eyes too, a joy from some unearthly great news, a joy impossible to take away.

What fire fuses together such polarities in one gaze? It is a miracle, the miracle of Seraphim's love.

When the image of Saint Seraphim arises and one begins telling the story of his life, it becomes clear that what matters is not what he said or did: words can be repeated and deeds described. The point is in his very being, a being that is greater than can be expressed here. You can only know him as he himself knew the world—with your heart.

There are holy places on our planet, where the forces of the stars, earth, air and water combine and make mighty spiritual accomplishments possible. Such a holy place was a mountain between the rivers Satis and Sarovka and a deserted Temnikovsky forest, with its cold springs, which remained unvisited for centuries by man's petty or unkind thoughts.

In the old days this place was inhabited by the Mordva people. Then it was taken by the Tatars. On the mountain where a monastery now stands, there was a fortified city. The Tatars left that place in the fourteenth century and since then it has become a desert, of which the chronicle says: "There is a great forest of mighty trees: oaks, pines and other growths. Many animals live in that forest: bears, lynxes, moose, foxes, martens; and along the rivers Satis and Sarov live beavers and otters. That place is not known by men, except by Mordva beekeepers." Not a single soul inhabited that place for three hundred years!

In the seventeenth century a monk came there and set up his cell on the rampart of the old settlement.

Some wondrous things he saw there at night. The sky opened up, the trees, water and grasses stood flooded with an indescribable light, and the ringing of many bells was heard.

Another elderly hermit who came after told a similar story, that at the feast of The Annunciation a great ringing shook the whole mountain. The mysterious ringing repeated more than once and the elder said, "Verily I believe this place is holy."

Once, some peasants came there to look for treasure, but all they found were seven equilateral crosses. Six of them were made of wood and the seventh was made of copper. After that the holy mountain stood deserted again for a long, long time...

In the year of 1706 a monk from the Arzamas District, Father Isaakiy, arrived there. He dug a cave for himself and for a long time wrestled with adversity all alone. Later on, his brethren joined him and a monastery was founded. When the first church was being built, the ringing of the invisible bells was heard again. The indescribable light was also seen again.

Life in the forest wilderness was austere. The brethren plowed and sowed, milled flour on a grindstone, wove their clothes and bast shoes. They wore sheepskins in winter and rough linen in summer. An infusion of raspberries, mint and honey was their only special treat reserved for festive occasions. Love and a heroic human spirit lived between them.

Life was not without calamities there. Twice, robbers attacked at night, looted the church and tortured monks at the stake; fires ravaged the monastery, informers accused the brethren of collaborating with dissenters. Eventually Father Isaakiy, in the schema Ioann, was falsely accused, arrested, and died in St. Petersburg's prison. These were tumultuous times, times of the reign of Anna Ioannovna.§ It is known that in 1775, the year of the great famine, the brethren fed people from nearby villages and were ready to starve with them when food supplies ran out.

In 1778, on the eve of the feast of The Entry of the Most Holy Theotokos into the Temple, there was an all-night vigil in the Sarov monastery. Among the worshippers stood Prokhor, a tall young man with blond hair, and blue eyes that radiated a quiet joy. He had come from afar, walking the remote paths of the autumn forest to attend the celebration. The monastery was filled with singing: "The most pure temple of the Savior, the most precious bridal chamber, the Virgin, the sacred treasury of God's glory, enters today into the house of the Lord, bringing with her the Grace of the Spirit Divine."

---

§ *Anna Ioanovna*, Empress of Russia from 1730 to 1740. Anna's reign is often referred to as "the dark era."

It was a celebration of the great day of The Presentation, when a three-year-old Mary was brought into the temple and was led into the Holy of Holies by the high priest, in accordance with divine revelation.

As candles burned with golden light and the brethren chanted joyfully, so did Prokhor's soul ignite in joyful singing: "O, Holy Virgin bringing Grace."

Prokhor (later called Seraphim) was born in Kursk on July 19, 1759. His Father, Isidor Moshnin, was a wealthy merchant who owned brick factories and took contracts to build houses and churches.

He was building the Kursk Cathedral designed by Rastrelli,¶ but died before completing construction and entrusted it to his wife. Prokhor was three years old at the time. Once, when he was seven years old, his mother took him with her to the construction site, where he fell from the bell tower but he miraculously remained unscathed.

It is interesting that similar cases of falling from heights and escaping harm in childhood are found

---

¶ *Francesco Bartolommeo Rastrelli* (1700–1771) was an Italian architect who worked mainly in Russia. He developed a Late Baroque style, both sumptuous and majestic. His major works, including the Winter Palace in Saint Petersburg and the Catherine Palace in Tsarskoye Selo, are famed for their extravagant luxury and opulence of decoration.

in the biographies of other great personalities, who later in life were called to accomplish spiritual deeds. It is as if the experience is bestowed upon a person in order to awaken certain forces within them.

While the body, obeying the laws of physics, rushes down with accelerating speed and should be crushed, the spirit is not subjected to the same physical laws and has its own distinct life. Hence, the spirit overcomes the laws of the body. After such an experience, although unconsciously, a person steps into life differently. In the depths of their soul a voice says, "You should have died according to the laws of the flesh but you are alive by the will of the spirit. From now on you are dead to the laws of the body. You live for the spirit."

And such a person accepts life as a gift, a gift from the spirit, and offers their life as a gift to the spirit. The bond between the soul and the body in such a person is weaker, their soul is freer.

This experience must have affected Prokhor's mother greatly. She now looked upon her son's life as being protected and belonging to a higher power, and when Prokhor decided to enter monastic life, she gave him her blessing and gave him a big copper cross as a benediction. This copper cross was always worn by Saint Seraphim.

Three years after falling from the bell tower, Prokhor became severely ill and was deemed incurable. At that time he had a dream and in this dream the Mother of God visited him, promising to help. The boy shared this dream with his mother. Not long after, a procession carrying the wonder-working icon of Our Lady of the Sign passed by the Moshnins' house.** Prokhor was brought to the Icon for a blessing and a miraculous healing took place.

When something unexplainable yet obvious happens, we call it a miracle. The outer world is ruled by cause and effect, but in the world of the spirit the effect appears first, followed by the means of its attainment. It can be compared to building a bell tower. The roof comes first in a designer's mind but is the last to be built. In the higher worlds, everything is a miracle—the spirit manifests without an intermediary; in other words, without causes. Aims reign supreme in the world of the spirit, whereas our world is ruled by causes.

The more a human being is filled with spirit, the more miracles can happen in them and through them. To be miraculously restored to health is a direct effect of the spirit active in the body. In ancient

---

** *Our Lady of Kursk* (also the Kursk Root Icon of the Sign) is one of the most beloved and revered holy images in the history of Russian icons. It was discovered in a forest near Kursk circa 1295. The icon was preserved in the Black Hermitage of the Roots (Chornaya Korennaya Pustyn), an abbey founded on the spot of its discovery. It was regularly brought from the abbey to Kursk in a great procession involving thousands of peasants and pilgrims. This ceremony is depicted in the famous painting by Ilya Repin, Religious Procession in Kursk Province.

times, the sick were healed by those powerful in spirit, as the human body was not yet strongly hardened and was more sensitive and responsive to the influence of the spirit.

Disease represents a disruption of the order in which the forces of the human body act in unison with the world's forces. When man lived in harmony with nature and in peace with Mother Earth, he was divinely unaware of his separate will. In the time before the fall from paradise he did not know illness, which was born when the fire of an independent will was kindled in man, and he broke away from the natural order of things. Self-awareness and freedom were gained at the price of suffering. Harmony with nature and wholeness were broken.

What can mend that rift and restore man to health? Disease sprung from the spiritual, so the spiritual can also overcome it. When the spirit, having experienced freedom and self-consciousness freely, like a son, returns to the divine Mother, it has the power to restore what is broken.

And what can heal if not the essence, the image of that which is whole, of that which is pure and virtuous? The image of the Holy Mother restores the spirit to that lost pure state of being. The miracle works wonders and restores wholeness.

While in his sleep, Seraphim received spiritual help. It was expressed in a dream and manifested in reality by the "accidental" carrying of the Holy Icon past the Moshnins' house. The effect appeared in a dream; the means of its attainment came afterwards.

The paradisiacal vision of the Mother of God lived in the spirit of Saint Seraphim and a wondrous connection with the Most Holy Virgin illuminated his whole life. In this lies a great mystery, the unspoken truth of all Mother Russia.

"This one is of our own kind," She says of Seraphim, appearing to him afterwards. When the boy was well again, he resumed his studies. He was taught in the customary way merchant children were taught in eighteenth-century Russia. He learned to read and write from the Book of Hours, the Psalms and the Bible. He read religious books willingly. There was an attempt to engage him in business. His older brother had a shop where all sorts of goods for peasants were sold: harnesses, sandals, tar. Prokhor would go to the shop, but without joy. What brought him joy was getting up before the others and attending Matins and early Liturgy.

Everything in church was an image of the world his heart knew and loved. It was a world so entirely different from everyday life with its excesses and injustices that pained his heart. He would also go to have talks with one considered a fool, whose name is now forgotten. There was a deep connection between the child and this blessed one, who did not accept the ways and logic of this world and who kept faithful to a different truth, a truth that did not belong to this world. In this fool's awkward words, guileless eyes and gentle smile, Prokhor saw the light of divine wisdom, the wisdom that is madness before men.

When Prokhor decided to join the monastery a few years later, he encountered no obstacles from anybody. Five other merchants he knew wanted to go with him. There was a solemn custom of saying goodbye to one's ancestral home before departure. It was a custom in which everyone sat in silence. There was profound meaning in such silence, silence stretching between the old and the new life, the soul letting the new ripen within, listening to the will of the coming life, taking strength from it.

Another custom was that of kneeling before one's mother for a blessing, as an expression of a farewell to one's blood family, in whose bosom the spirit ripened and, once matured, separated like a fruit from a tree; and as an expression of gratitude to a mother for having built the temple of the body in which this spirit could develop to enter a new life.

Prokhor knelt before his mother who was holding a holy icon. He kissed the icon, received the blessing, and his mother placed a large copper cross on his chest.

First, Prokhor went to Kiev, where Russia was Christianized. His five companions came with him. He wanted to touch the holy relics of the early ascetics, pray in the temple of St. Sophia of the Wisdom of God, and seek advice and guidance from the prophetic hermit Dositheus. After Prokhor knelt before the old man and kissed his feet, he revealed his heart's desire and asked for advice. The old man sent him to Sarov: "Go, my child, and stay there. Through the grace of the Lord, that place will be your salvation, and you will complete your earthly journey there as well. Seek to always call upon the name of God—'Lord Jesus Christ, Son of God, have mercy upon me, a sinner!'—With this should be all your attention and instruction. Walking and sitting, at work and in church, standing everywhere, in every place, on coming and going, let this unceasing invocation be on your lips and in your heart. With it you will find peace, obtain spiritual and bodily purity, and the Holy Spirit, the source of all blessedness, will dwell in you and will direct your life in holiness, devotion and integrity. In Sarov, Father Pakhomiy is the abbot whose life is pleasing to God. He is a follower of our Anthony and Theodosius."

Father Pakhomiy was a former Kursk merchant acquainted with Prokhor's parents.

After his stay in Kiev, Prokhor returned to Kursk and lived at home for a few more months. He was in the shop every day, but did not engage in sales. Like someone belonging to a different world, he did not concern himself with business, but was visited by peasants, merchants and townspeople who came to talk to him about holy places, the saints and God's truth.

He was nineteen years old when, on the eve of the feast of the Entry of the Theotokos into the Temple, he came to the Sarov monastery and was warmly greeted by Father Pakhomiy, who entrusted him to the care of the elder Iosif.

Some people may say that the life of a monk is an extreme selfishness, for when a man, detaching himself from the world, immerses himself into his inner life and thinks only of the salvation of his own soul, what good is it to others? Is he not robbing the world of its useful member, and depriving himself of the gifts of life? But such reasoning would only indicate a superficial view of things.

We will not speak here of such a monastic life, where everything is turned into appearance, into a ritual, where natural human experiences are taken away from people and are not replaced by higher, spiritual ones; where, therefore, worldly feelings have no natural outcome and live in secret; where idleness, curiosity and pretense are especially active. Such a life is a falsehood, a monstrosity, and a violation of nature.

Here we will speak of the life of a monk embarking on a spiritual path following a true calling.

What is the purpose of his life?

Such a person, detaching himself from all the things the outer world can give him, replaces it with something else—an inner life. He makes his soul independent of the external world, of external impressions.

He devotes himself continually to certain inner experiences, repeating in his soul certain prayers, and by doing so he gives his soul a strong foundation. An inwardly strengthened soul, having obtained its composition and structure, becomes a soul body which can perceive the spiritual world, just as our physical body, by virtue of its composition and structure, perceives the external world. Yes, that is exactly how it is. And this soul mental body is built by a person himself through determined and intensive inner work. This is called spiritual doing (*Hesychasm*).††

Through prayer, the content of thoughts and feelings that fill the soul no longer depend on time and place. These eternal feelings and thoughts fill the soul to such an extent that there is no more room for the transitory. They nourish that eternal part of the human being which in ordinary life appears to be dormant. This immortal core of the spirit begins to be aware of itself and one becomes an awake participant of the spiritual world. He begins to see and hear clearly in the spirit world. He enters into interaction with the beings of the spirit world, with the hierarchies of the spiritual forces.

The first condition for this must be an inner purification. A monk is to keep a strict watch over

---

†† *Hesychasm* is a contemplative monastic practice in Eastern Christian traditions in which stillness (*hēsychia*) is sought through uninterrupted Jesus Prayer.

himself, lest his soul world be clouded by personal desires and passions. It has to become quiet and clear in his soul, his inner world brought to silence. Then in this silence, in this clarity, the spiritual mysteries underlying the whole external world will be revealed to him, and he will become a transparent vessel for the Holy Spirit.

Devotion, obedience, fasting, and other exercises are only the instruments for bringing about inner strengthening and purification.

Obedience is a voluntary renunciation of one's will, and therefore it is not a violation of the will.

By voluntarily surrendering his will, a person only eliminates its external manifestation, while its inner force is strengthened by this renunciation. The primary basis of the will, the core of it, must remain inviolable, as the holy of holies. The will learns how not to want for itself (how not to want what it wants).

The same is true with fasting. Fasting strengthens the will, which seeks to free the soul from its dependence upon the external world, and makes available for the spirit those forces that would have been used to satisfy the physical.

There is a universal law: all new comes through the sacrifice of the old, and the highest —through the sacrifice of the lowest. You must push off the bottom step with your foot to reach the top step. Very often at the core of any development, any unfolding of greatness and beauty, is suffering and sacrifice.

But usually, people do not know why they return again and again to suffer on earth. They do not know to what spiritual goal divine providence leads them through suffering, and therefore they suffer unwillingly.

Only those who have embarked on the path of spiritual quest willingly take upon themselves hardship and suffering, thus helping to realize the will of God in themselves and in the world.

Pain, both spiritual and bodily, all pain, is a delay in the manifestation of forces; and if there is a delay, there is also an accumulation of these forces, and their transformation into new and higher ones.

"A seed, if it does not die, will not come to life." From such consciousness arose the ascetic ideal of the early monastics. They mortified their flesh by keeping vigil, fasting and self-flagellation.

But we must never forget that times change, that the ascetic ideal given to mankind in antiquity cannot be an ideal of ours. All of life was different, and man in his mental and physical constitution was different, and the world was different. This is something we must never forget. What was beautiful and necessary at one time would now be a harmful and unhealthy deviation. The highest eternal goal remains the same, but the means and ways must change with time.

In those days, in order to make the body a perfect instrument of the spirit, it was necessary to gain mastery of it with such harsh external measures. In our time a more inward work on the soul is possible, which will gradually spiritualize and transform the body from within. Instead of the sphere of the visible and the physical, sacrifices become internal and invisible. The struggle with oneself is transferred into the inner realm, but this invisible feat is still the same feat.

Saint Seraphim lived at a time when those wishing to embark on the spiritual path had to leave the world, go to a monastery and mortify their flesh. He turned all his inner ardor into a feat of incredible strength so that he could die in Christ and rise again in the Spirit.

Prokhor's obedience consisted in serving the elder Joseph, helping in the bakery, in the wafery, in carpentry work; with special love he carved crosses out of cypress wood for the worshipers.

He was known as Prokhor the carpenter and he also shared in the work of the brethren by felling and cutting wood with them. In his cell, he read the Gospels, the Epistles of the Apostles, the Six Days of St. Basil the Great,‡‡ the Discourses of St. Macarius,§§ and the Philokalia.¶¶

Whenever Prokhor was free, he went into the woods to fulfill his prayer rule, that is, a series of prayers given to him by the elder.

The Jesus Prayer, "Lord Jesus Christ, Son of God, have mercy on me, a sinner," was first spoken, and then expressed with a thought, and finally not even with a thought, but with all the powers of the soul. He lived with this prayer unceasingly, with every heartbeat. It was like the very breath of his being. It was his life. It remained his main prayer until his last days.

In this prayer the soul appeals to its higher self as to the Lord. This higher, divine element in the soul is the Son of God. It is that Being Who lives in every soul, but Who only once incarnated in its

---

‡‡ *Hexameron* is the genre of theological treatise that describes God's work on the six days of creation or to the six days of creation themselves. Most often these theological works take the form of commentaries on Genesis. Saint Basil wrote an early and influential series of homilies around 370 AD which figure as the earliest extant Hexameron.

§§ *St. Macarius The Egyptian* (295–392 AD) was among the most authoritative Desert Fathers of Egypt, and a disciple of St. Anthony the Great. He is considered by the Church to be one of the founding fathers of monasticism.

¶¶ *The Philokalia* (φιλοκαλία: "love of the beautiful") a collection of texts written between the fourth and fifteenth centuries by spiritual masters of the mystical hesychast tradition of the Eastern Orthodox Church.

fullness in Jesus Christ; and it is only through Him, through His becoming man on earth, through His death and resurrection, that men can find Him in their souls. To Him the soul cries out for mercy. As by grace the Son of God appeared on earth, so in the human "I" He is revealed by grace and as grace itself, as an abundance of love. And when the soul asks for mercy, it does so not out of fear of the transgressor, but it pleads for a gift of grace and love, for in the Son of God everything is a gift. When He is in the soul, He takes all things upon Himself, He envelops everything in His abundance. For He did not come to judge, but to give us life, and to give it abundantly. This is what the soul asks for, opening itself to receive the gift, breathing in the Spirit. But it feels sinful, not whole, unclean, because it cannot merge with God, because it is bound and blinded by transient things. And the soul grieves, longing for Christ, from whom it is separated, as a bride longs for her bridegroom and laments, and prepares for herself white garments, breathing in God.

"Lord Jesus Christ, Son of God, have mercy upon me, a sinner!" Thus, he prayed in his cell, in the church and in the forest; in the quiet and resinous forest, where, together with him, the trees were doing their forest prayer, surrendering themselves to the sun, taking the solar forces into the night of the earth, praying for the black earth, for the earth-widow, breathing in the sun.

In his twenty-first year, Prokhor fell ill and was sick for three years. His body became swollen. The doctors could not understand his illness.

The elders Pakhomiy and Isaiah, his confessor, were with him at all times. They feared for his life, and at last, preparing him for death, they gave him Holy Communion. Then, in an indescribable light he saw the Mother of God near him. With Her were the Apostles Peter and John, and turning Her face to John, She said, "This one is of Our kind." She put her right hand on Prokhor's head, and with her other hand touched him with a staff. He told about this vision only later, and for a long time his fast recovery remained a mystery to all.

After being a novice for eight years, Prokhor took monastic vows, and was given the name Seraphim, which means "fiery." Soon he was ordained a hierodeacon, and for six years he served almost continuously, spending even part of the night in the church. His vigor was great.

The visible world was becoming more and more transparent to him, and another world, invisible to most people, but real and true, was coming through. He saw young men in gold or white robes serving with him in the church. They sang with the congregation, but their voices could not be compared to anything else. "My heart was like wax and was melting with inexpressible joy." This is what he said, but he remembered only how he entered the church and how he left it.

Once, on Holy Thursday, Father Pakhomiy was celebrating the liturgy with Hierodeacon Seraphim. After the Small Entry, which depicts the entrance to the higher spiritual worlds, when a priest prays, "May our entry be accompanied by the holy angels, serving us and praising Your goodness," Seraphim cried out, "O Lord, deliver the blessed and hear us…" and, turning to the people and making a sign with his orarion, finished, "…for ever and ever." With this his face changed. He fell silent and remained motionless. He saw a sunbeam shining on him, and Christ approaching through the air from the western gates of the church, surrounded as if by a swarm of bees, by angels, archangels, cherubim and seraphim. He approached the pulpit and, lifting up His hands, blessed the people and the servers. Then He entered His own local image on the right side of the royal gates and was transfigured. The light from His Glory flooded the whole church. Seraphim was led by his arms to the altar. He stood there motionless for three hours, turning from pale to glowing. When he came to himself, he told his elders about the vision. "I," he said, "who am earth and ashes, beholding the Lord Jesus Christ, was honored with a special blessing from Him. My heart purely rejoiced, and was enlightened, in the sweetness of love for the Lord."

At the age of thirty-four, Seraphim was ordained a hieromonk in Tambov. He spent all his days in the monastery at the services, and at night he went to his solitary cell in the woods to pray. He longed for complete solitude, and a year later the tutelary Pakhomiy, when dying, blessed Seraphim to a life in the wilderness.

Having buried his favorite elder, Seraphim retired to his remote hermitage. There, on the bank of the Sarovka River, in a dense forest, where green linden trees grew intermingled with giant pines, five miles from the monastery, he had a hut with a stove, a shed and a porch. He chopped wood, worked in his small garden and his beehouse. Other hermits who lived in the same forest could hear his voice in the forest silence, singing "The World's Glory" or "To the Desolate Unceasing Divine Longing Be Granted." Sometimes they happened to see how, while he was working, his shovel suddenly fell out of his hands, his face became inexplicably radiant, and he would stand motionless for hours, beholding mysteries of which he perhaps has never told anyone.

On Sundays, Seraphim went to the monastery, where he was given dried bread, his only sustenance, but this he shared with the beasts and birds of the forest. Even snakes and a big bear came to him. The elder fed and stroked the bear, which would retreat into the forest at Seraphim's command.

And that was only a hundred years ago! The legend tells us about a nun who was very afraid of that big bear, but was able to feed him nevertheless, under Seraphim's guidance.

This image is a memory of the most distant paradisiacal times of our earth, when beast trustingly approached man as his older brother to whom he had ceded primacy. More precisely, it is both—a memory and a pledge for the future.

Seraphim's prophetic heart burned for every creature, and it knew the mystery of the relationship between man and beast, knew what man owed to a beast and how he was responsible before it, knew the innocence of a beast's passions and the hopelessness of its suffering. The beast's instinct recognized in Seraphim the spirit that would set him free, the love that would deliver it. Is not the man who frees himself by voluntary suffering the liberator of the world? Here is how the Apostle Paul speaks about it: "...I consider that all difficulties and sufferings of the present age are trivial compared with the light-power of the world of spirit which will reveal itself. All around us creation waits with great longing that the sons of God shall begin to shine forth in mankind. Creation has become transitory, not through its own doing, but because of him who, becoming transitory himself, dragged it down with him, and therefore everything in it is full of longing for the future. For the breath of freedom will also waft through the kingdoms of creation; the tyranny of transitory existence will cease. When the sphere of the Spirit grows bright, unfreedom will be replaced by the freedom which is intended for all God's offspring. We know that the whole of creation suffers and sighs in the pangs of a new birth until the present day..." (Rom. VIII, 18–22).

Seraphim loved and felt for animals as our poor lesser brothers, deprived of higher consciousness, but not deprived of suffering. Did they not submit to this condition in order that man might receive the spirit from above, that is, become a son of God? For, as has been said before, the highest is achieved by the sacrifice of the lowest, and is not the beast such an innocent sacrifice in the process of the world's development? Then the first duty of man, liberated "into the freedom of the glory of the children of God," is to liberate the creature.

If in a single human life this liberating love is realized through the victory of the spirit, then the path to the earth has been opened for love. The kingdom of God will come to earth through souls who have made room for it. Seraphim feeding the bear is a reality. It is the truth that laughs at our commonplace truth, making the impossible possible!

The challenge of the spiritual quest in the wilderness is great. Man is left entirely alone with his soul. As he goes deeper into himself, he sees himself as a battleground on which different forces clash. In the soul world, feelings and thoughts are beings. In social interactions with other people, these beings of the soul-world are expressed by man in feelings, words and deeds. In solitude there is no outlet for them. But the more powerful and vivid they appear before a disciplined self-awareness, the more merciless is their assault on the soul and the struggle against them. They appear in various guises as external enemies and fight against the spirit seeking to be free of them. Seraphim said, warning against the dangers of desert life, "In monasteries monks wrestle with adversary forces as with doves, but in the desert—as with lions and leopards."

All the entities of our soul-world, which we experience in life as our feelings and thoughts, inseparable from ourselves and belonging to us, are seen by the spiritual "I" of man as something that comes from without and seeks to exhaust itself in him. His spirit has, as it were, built a solid fortress in his soul. What he used to call his "I", now, from the point of view of that high spiritual fortress, is no longer an "I". He sees himself as a battlefield for all kinds of forces. And without identifying them with himself, he sees them in images, sometimes terrifying. He encounters the entire world's evil forces because he is a part of the world. He is a part of the whole world because the human being is a center of all the forces acting in the world. That is why one who frees himself is the liberator of the world. The higher, the stronger the spirit of a man, the more terrifying the mysteries and beings that are revealed to him. When asked by a lay man about evil spirits, Seraphim replied with a smile, "They are vile. As it is impossible for a sinner to look at the light of an angel, so it is terrifying to see demons, because they are vile."

One only has to look at St. Seraphim's eyes to see that even on poor portraits, those eyes, narrowed from concentration, tell us what terrifying knowledge of the world he carried in his soul, and that his eyes contemplated not only the heavenly lights, but also the very horror of darkness.

So, what can defeat the dark forces?

It is up to the individual to surrender to these forces or to make them serve the light. To do this, he must open himself to the light, that is, he must overcome his separateness and let the "I" that is one with Christ live in him.

Dark, inhibiting forces have their purpose in the world as a hindrance, as an opposition from which one gains strength. By realizing their true purpose, man becomes free from them and frees them from their dreadful lot. When man dies to his lower self, when he realizes that everything but the divine is an illusion and a deception, that he is nothing, and only that "I am" which is one with Christ is truth; when, like St. Paul, he can say, "Not I, but Christ in me," then he is freed from the dark powers and frees them unto the light. Ultimate humility is the sign of such freedom. And when the onslaught of dark forces reached the greatest strength in the soul of

St. Seraphim, he, in utter humility, in the realization of his worthlessness, began to climb a big rock in the forest at night, and, raising his hands to heaven, prayed in the words of the tax collector, "God, be merciful to me, a sinner," and during the day in his cell, kneeling on the rock he also kept there, he prayed in the same position. And so he prayed for a thousand days and a thousand nights.

Only before his death did Seraphim talk about this. And when they marveled at his strength, he said, "When there is humility in the heart, God is also with us."

In his tenth year in the woods, Seraphim was attacked by three men, who thought that the devotees were bringing him a lot of money. Seraphim was extraordinarily strong by nature. He had an axe in his hands and could have easily defended himself, but he threw the axe on the ground, folded his arms on his chest and said, "Do whatever you want." They tied him up and beat him nearly to death.

Barely alive he reached Sarov the next day, and when he showed up for Mass, everyone was terrified. His hair was clotted with blood, and his clothes were stuck to his wounds. For eight days he lay without sleep and without food in great suffering. Doctors were summoned. Three doctors and three nurses from Arzamas conferred about him in Latin, but he heard nothing. He was having a vision of the Blessed

Virgin surrounded by glory, dressed in purple, standing before him with Peter and John. "Why are you laboring?" She said to the assembled men. "This one is of Our kind." Seraphim was filled with great joy; he refused the help of the doctors and soon he was able to eat bread and cabbage and he started to get well.

The bandits were found. They turned out to be a neighbor's servants. They were to be punished severely, but Seraphim begged on their behalf, and threatened to leave Sarov if his request were not granted. Later on, the robbers came to him with repentance themselves. Seraphim was already crooked from an oak tree which once had fallen on him. Now he was so bent from the beatings that he could not walk unless he leaned on an axe or a hoe.

For three more years Seraphim lived in the hermitage as before. Father Pakhomiy was dead. After Pakhomiy father Joseph, who was Seraphim's first elder, also died and his second confessor after Pakhomiy, father Isaiah, died too. With these three, everything to which he was attached on earth died for Seraphim.

And everything in him of a personal and human nature suffered deeply. He was forty-eight years old at the time. He was alone in the world. His soul was longing. More and more he longed for a single and imperishable truth. He wanted to tame the sorrow in his soul, he wanted to erase that part in himself that was a mere personality, he wanted to keep silent and to let God speak in him.

Thus, he became a silent man.

No more was the door of his cell open, nor did he answer anyone's call. Whenever he encountered a man in the woods, he would fall with his face on the ground and would not get up until they moved on.

He was not seen in the monastery.

Once a week a novice monk brought food to Seraphim. In winter the snow-covered hermitage was barely accessible. It was quiet all around in the thick woods. The novice would knock on the door: "Lord Jesus Christ, Son of God, have mercy on me, a sinner!"

"Amen," the elder would answer him, and the door would open. Seraphim would stand with his hands folded and his eyes fixed on the ground, and at his feet would be a basket into which the novice would place the food.

It went on like this for three years. The monks started to worry about Seraphim's not receiving the Holy Communion, and they decided to offer him to come to the monastery on feast days only, and if his aching legs prevented him from coming, then to move back to his old cell. The novice monk who brought food to Seraphim was instructed to tell the elder of the proposal. Quietly the old man listened to the offer to come back, and the next time, he silently followed the novice to Sarov. This is how after sixteen years of solitude, Seraphim returned to his old cell, and this time he completely withdrew himself from the outer world.

In a hallway next to Seraphim's cell stood an oak coffin which he made for himself. All he had in his cell were an icon and a tree stump, he never lit a fire to warm up the cell, and his only food was cabbage, oatmeal and water. Every time a novice monk brought food, the kneeling old man, his face covered with a towel, accepted it in reverent silence as a precious gift. Very often people assembled around Seraphim's cell to listen to him pondering aloud about the Gospels.

Nobody saw Seraphim during the day and only at night could he be seen carrying wood while reciting the Jesus Prayer. On every feast day Seraphim received a Holy Communion in his cell.

And so in this way another five years went by. Later Seraphim said, "Silence is the mystery of the age to come, while words are the instruments of this world." When he was later asked why, having adopted silence, he deprived his brothers of spiritual instruction, he answered, "Gregory the Theologian said, 'It is wonderful to praise God with words, but it is better if a man purifies himself for God.'"

"In deep silence God speaks His word," said another teacher.

We may ask, "What is the word of God and the word of man, of which it is said that 'it is the instrument of this world?'"

A long time ago, the word was very different from what it has become today, today the word is more formal: through the gift of the word bestowed on man, God named all His creations, and the names given were their true names. The name contained real spiritual forces present in the thing that was named and it embodied the soul of the thing and therefore belonged to it. The word was the creative power of God that gave life to nature, the divine will resounded in it, and the elements obeyed it. But the word has lost this power because it has lost the truth. It is now not the divine will that is revealed in the word, not the essence of things expressed through it, but it has become an instrument of man who has fallen away from God, has begun to serve his separate will, following his own cravings and desires. Man has forgotten the original holiness of the word, and the word has become a lie. A spoken word is no longer followed by a deed.

How can the word's original holiness be restored? How can it be liberated from the world in which it has become a lie, so that it may become God's word again? And what is no longer a lie in the world? Man himself, the whole man, visible and external, withdrawn into his senses and egoism, is he not a shattered reflection of truth, a guise and a falsehood?

The word of man has become a lie, and his face has become a deception.

So, Seraphim wanted, with all the might of his eternal spirit, to erase this falsehood from the face of the earth. When he met a man in the forest, he fell face down on the ground. When he opened his door, he covered his face with a towel. When for fifteen years no mortal heard a word from him, he was erasing his own falsehood from the earth.

After ten years of silence, Seraphim opened his cell, but he did not break his silence. One could enter his cell and see him reading and praying.

His face had become a countenance, a light condensed into a human appearance. His eyes had become wellsprings of compassion and his lips had become a revelation of the word.

After five years, he began to answer questions and give spiritual advice. It was a tender love song of God's simple truth. And after another five years, the Mother of God instructed him to come out of his hermitage and to receive all who needed to see him. At that time, he had seven years of earthly life left.

Seraphim was sixty-six years old when, after thirty-odd years of seclusion, in 1825, he opened the door of his cell to all, and would see people from early morning until late into night. In his cell, with its windows overlooking a field, there were sandbags on which he slept; but in his later years, he slept kneeling, resting his elbows on the floor and supporting his head with his hands. His cell was never heated, but it was kept hot by numerous icon lamps and many candles burning on round wooden trays, for the repose of those souls for whom Seraphim prayed. He stood in the candles' golden glow as a kind of spirit, the white-haired old man in his white robe and his mantle, himself like a lighted candle burning for both worlds. Both the living and the dead sought help from the light of his soul and his prayers were heard and needed in both worlds.

The simple and the noble, the virtuous and the sinful, all came to him.

"My joy!" This is how he greeted everyone and at every season of the year he said, "Christ is risen!"

The abundance of Seraphim's love and joy, earned through selfless sacrifice, filled the cracks in suffering human souls. When Seraphim spoke, through his words, he offered people around him his own living power, his own heart, his very being—he offered himself freely.

One's divine image, originating in God, the image that had been lost, was restored in the hearts he spoke to. In everyone, Seraphim saw their true, untainted, primordial countenance, a countenance that will be revealed at the end of time. This ability to see the inner light in every person, regardless of "the dust from the journey," was a source of tremendous joy and delight for Seraphim.

Was it not possible for Seraphim to see all the evil and darkness in human souls? Did he not see in people their egotism, dwelling in the depths of their souls and of which they were not aware? Yes, he saw it and he saw more than that, more of what was of a temporary and transient nature. In each of these souls he saw and loved God, Who one day shall shine through all darkness.

Just as the sun, seeing a small seed buried in the black earth, sends its warmth and light to it, prompting the seed to sprout and to grow into a beautiful flowering plant, so does love: it sees in another, through the darkness and smallness of the temporal, the current, that which slumbers in them, as a plant slumbers in a seed; and, seeing it, love calls it to awaken, summons it before the Divine Light which reveals the beauty of the soul. As the earth greens and blossoms under the power of the sun's love, so souls can blossom illumined by the light and fire of another person's loving heart.

"God is fire," said Saint Seraphim. "God is love."

Discernment is love too, and it is born out of compassion. The soul that is no longer closed in on itself expands into the world, taking more and more beings into its sphere, bringing its consciousness into them, merging its heart with their hearts, listening to their hearts as to its own. When a house is quiet inside, you can hear the voices outside. This is how a quiet soul hears the souls of others.

When people came to Seraphim for confession, he would often tell them of their transgressions before they confessed. He also saw their past and warned them about the future.

Why are the past and the future open to spiritual sight?

As we already mentioned, in the spiritual world, we first see the divine goal, and then the ways and means that the spirit chooses to realize the goal, which, to our everyday consciousness appear as causes. When an experienced builder sees the blueprint of a building, he can tell how it will be built, and when he sees a building, he can tell how its construction was carried out.

In the external world, events move towards the spiritual goal. The present is born spiritually out of the future as the means to an end. The visible world is a reflection of the spirit, and, as in the mirror the right is a reflection of the left, so the former is reflected in the outer life by the latter. To one awake in the spirit, the future is open and it appears as fulfilled.

There is no un-freedom or fatalism in this. For in the future, those goals are realized, which the eternal and immortal "I" of man sets for itself, leading one through all the sufferings and through many lifetimes, so that one can overcome one's previous flaws and learn what one did not know before. The lower self of man is blind. It suffers involuntarily and laments, not knowing that this path is chosen by means of good will. Seeing in a person his higher self in the spiritual world, and seeing a person here in their becoming, Saint Seraphim was able to behold their entire earth journey with all of life's possibilities and all of its inevitabilities.

With the superabundance of spirit that was earned by his suffering, Seraphim relieved some of a person's destined burden, took it upon his own soul by giving counsel and by delivering from ailments.

After each confession, he would kiss a person with the words, "Christ is risen!" and he would always say it at at any time of the year, not only at Easter. Seraphim knew the suffering in men and in all created beings. This burden was the cross he carried patiently and he never spoke of it. He spoke only of the resurrection, allowing his love to flow abundantly into all suffering creation.

We can tell from the look in Seraphim's eyes on the few remaining portraits of him, of the cross that he carried.

He would greet each person as a brother, delighting in the brotherly spirit, often bowing to the ground, and lovingly kissing his visitors' hands.

When Seraphim left the hermitage, his health was poor. He suffered from headaches and aching feet. He began to go into the forest to a nearby hermitage. There was a dried-up spring there. An icon of John the Theologian stood on a post near it. At that time the dried-up spring began to run again. Seraphim blessed it, bestowing on it a healing power. By this spring the elder would work. He collected pebbles from the river Sarovka and laid the spring with them. Nearby he planted onions and potatoes. A log cabin was built for him here where he could take a rest from the heat; two years later a windowless cell was constructed in the log cabin. Every day between two and four o'clock in the morning, the old man walked from the monastery to the nearby hermitage in his white robe and a wrinkled cap, leaning on a hoe. He carried a bag of stones, sand, and the book of Gospels on top of them. When asked why he took such pains, he replied, "I am tormenting the one who torments me."

Crowds waited for him along his path from the hermitage to the church, especially when he partook of Holy Communion. When the sick came for Seraphim's blessings, he offered them dried bread and gave them water from his spring to drink. He also asked them to bathe in the water of the spring.

The first person Seraphim healed was a neighboring landowner, Mikhail Vasilyevich Manturov. Seraphim was still living in isolation when Manturov's men brought their master to him, suffering from a severe ailment of the legs. Doctors could not help, and Manturov had to quit his military service and settle at his estate.

"Why have you come here? You want to see humble Seraphim?" the old man greeted him. When the sick man begged for healing, Seraphim asked him three times if he had faith in God. Manturov believed in God. Seraphim left him in the parlor, seated on the coffin, while he himself went to his cell to pray. After a while he came back, kneeled before Manturov, and, rubbing his legs with consecrated oil, said, "By the Lord's grace bestowed upon me, you are the first one to receive this cure." Then he asked Manturov to stand up, filled his pockets with dried bread, and told him to go to the monastery. The healed man bowed down before him, but Seraphim said sternly, "Is it Seraphim's business to make one dead or to revive? What are you saying, my friend?! This is the work of God alone."

On the advice of Seraphim, Manturov entered into voluntary poverty in thanksgiving to God for his recovery. Yet Manturov was very unhappy, first on account of his Lutheran wife, who could not reconcile herself to such a fate, then from the slanders and persecutions of others. However, he managed to humble his fiery and proud temper and, out of devotion to Seraphim, he became a faithful assistant to the elder, especially in everything that concerned Diveevo.

Diveevo, a women's monastery some eight miles from Sarov, was Seraphim's most beloved child. It was founded by Mother Alexandra Melgunova, whom Seraphim called "a great woman." There is a portrait of her in which her pensive eyes look into the distance from under a fur-trimmed hat; her sculpted eyebrows, fine nose and her entire appearance are reminiscent of an icon. There is so much tender, thoughtful Russian beauty in her austere face, full of wisdom and will. In one hand she holds a rosary, in the other a staff. She was a widow and owned many estates, but she left it all and wandered through Russia, visiting holy places, serving and secretly doing charitable work.

Mother Alexandra Melgunova, founder of Diveevo
Unknown illustrator, from the 1913 Russian edition.

In Kiev's Frolovsky monastery she had a vision. The Mother of God instructed her to go north and, after appearing to her a second time in Diveevo, told her to found a monastery there. Her spiritual endeavor was great. When Father Pakhomiy was anointing the dying Mother Alexandra Melgunova, she asked him not to abandon her "Diveevo orphans," and Seraphim, at the time a hierodeacon, was present there too. Eventually Father Pakhomiy entrusted Diveevo to him.

There is a certain mystery hidden within the Diveevo monastic community which the future may reveal. Seraphim said that the Abbess of the monastery was the Mother of God Herself and that there was not a single stone in the monastery which he, humble Seraphim, had not laid at Her command, and that Diveevo would be the spiritual bulwark of the future Russia. Once, while he was in the woods near Sarov, the Heavenly Queen appeared to the venerable Seraphim. She gave Her blessing to found a community of maidens, to build a monastery there along with a mill and to line it with a Holy Kanavka (a dug-out ditch), which would be made by following the footsteps of the Most Holy Virgin. When the Antichrist reigns over the whole earth, the Holy Kanavka would rise up to the sky and the Antichrist would not be able to cross it. Many things Seraphim did for Diveevo, whether it was buying land or building a church, had special mysterious meanings, which were inexplicable.

One day the elder summoned Manturov, took a wooden stake, and, crossing himself, kissed the stake. Manturov did the same. Then, bowing before Manturov, he asked him to go to Diveevo, and, having counted off so many steps from the window of the Kazan church, to drive the stake into the ground. In addition, having never been to Diveevo himself, Seraphim precisely pointed out to him the grooves and glades that would be found there. When Manturov returned, having fulfilled his errand, Seraphim again bowed silently before him and remained very joyful all throughout that day. For a whole year, he did not mention anything about it, then in 1824 he summoned Manturov again and handed him four stakes, kissing them in the same manner, crossing himself and asking Manturov to do the same, then bowing down before Manturov, he indicated where to drive them into the ground at four corners in relation to the first one.

Four years later, on this spot a mill was built and it became the breadwinner for the sisters at Diveevo. A unique community, consisting of twelve maidens, was initiated at this mill by Seraphim. The nuns followed a special prayer rule, which, according to the words of the elder, was given to them by the Mother of God herself. Their prayer schedule was full and strict, but Seraphim saw to it that they did not exhaust themselves, were always nourished and happy, and that there was no spirit of despondency among them.

The elder treated the nuns with special affection.

"Have you seen my mill maidens, my dear?" he asked a certain woman.

"I have, father."

"Have you seen the bees, my dear?"

"How could I not, father?"

"You see, just like bees circle around the queen bee, and the queen bee never leaves them, so my maidens of Diveevo, exactly like the bees, will always be with the Mother of God."

Two female characters are connected with Saint Seraphim in Diveevo's mystery. One is Manturov's younger sister, Elena Vasilyevna, who was a great beauty. She wore black braids wrapped around her head and her dark eyes shone with joy and determination. At the age of seventeen she became a bride. A year later an inexplicable upheaval took place in her life. Nobody seemed to know, nor did she know herself, why she had suddenly refused her fiancé, who loved her, and whom she had loved very much before. Soon after, she became ill with nervous fever when visiting a neighboring estate. On her way back home, she had a disturbing vision, after which she decided to join a convent. The following took place at the post station*** : the servants were preparing tea in the common room, while she remained alone in the carriage and dozed off. When a servant came

---

*** house or inn with a stable that provided services for travelers and mail carriers

to get her, he saw her standing by the open door of the carriage leaning backward, frozen stiff with terror. She was carried inside the room and a priest was sent for. The terror stayed with her all day. She had a vision of all the adversity that separates man from God; all the selfish, dark forces were hovering above her in the form of a hideous black fire-breathing serpent. It was a reflection of her lower nature.

Soon, she went to Seraphim and expressed to him her desire to join the monastery. But he would always tell her about her forthcoming marriage, for which she should prepare herself: "While your fiancé is away, do not be discouraged, but be brave. You will need three years to prepare yourself, and when you are ready he will come and will bring you a ring." She cried and grumbled, not understanding what he was saying. "And I will tell you another thing, my joy—when you are in labor, do not be so fast at everything, for you are too fast, my joy, and that is not good; be slower, do everything slowly," and the elder showed her how she should lift everything carefully, how she should walk. "If you go like this, you will be safely delivered!" He was speaking to her about her spiritual birth, about the birth of the higher self. And when she was twenty years old, he told her that he was accepting her as a nun in Diveevo. "That is what a bridegroom is, my joy."

Elena Vasilyevna possessed a mighty will and followed her path unwaveringly, giving herself to the spiritual exploit with all the strength of her soul.

The spiritual world was revealing itself to her often suddenly, and Seraphim had to protect her from frightening visions. It was not without good reason that he held her back for three long years. She was amiable and well educated, and, like her brother, Mikhail Manturov, assisted Seraphim in dealing with the outside world in all Diveevo affairs. The starets called her the head Mistress of the Diveevo girls, to which she humbly but firmly objected.

When she was twenty-seven years old, he summoned her, saying, "My joy, you have always been obedient to me." She said that she would obey him now as well. "It is time for your brother to die, but he is needed for Diveevo. You are to die for Mikhail Vasilyevich."

And she said. "Give me your blessings, Father."

He spoke to her of the sweetness of death, when she suddenly said, "Father, I'm afraid of death."

"My joy, why should we be afraid of death? An everlasting joy awaits us there."

She bade her farewell to Seraphim, but on his doorstep, she fell down. Seraphim gave her holy water to drink.

Returning home, she lay down, saying, "Now I shall rise no more." Before dying she experienced beautiful visions and she died on the eve of Pentecost.

Seraphim told the sisters who were away in Sarov to go home, saying, "Hurry, hurry, return to the monastery. Your great mistress has gone to the Lord there."

"Why do you weep? You should rejoice!" he said to her apprentice, and his cell neighbor heard him repeating, "They don't understand anything! They weep! If only they saw how her soul flew! Like a bird it took to the air and Cherubim and Seraphim cleared the way for her!"

There is another remarkable character that shines beside the elder Seraphim: Maria. She belonged to a peasant family and came to Sarov with her sister, a nun from Diveevo. It was in 1822 on the feast of the Presentation to the Temple. She was thirteen years old at the time, a tall, slender girl with long golden hair, golden eyebrows and golden eyelashes. Her face was delicately blushed, and her blue eyes were of an extraordinary beauty and austerity. Seraphim asked her not to go back home to her village and to join the community of sisters at Diveevo, which she did. Maria was mostly silent. She only quietly answered questions. Seraphim called her to him more often than the others and told her about his revelations, of the mysteries of Russia, which she preserved in her heart.

She died at the age of nineteen. At the hour of her death, Seraphim wept and said to his monk neighbor, "Maria has departed, and I feel so sorry that I weep all the time."

"She took ascetic vows," he said to her sister, "and was given the name Martha, when she became an ascetic nun. As a nun, she had her mantle, and her stole, and I gave her my prayer cap."

She was laid in a solid oak coffin which came from Seraphim. A green velvet cap embroidered with gold was placed on her loose hair, in her hands they put a rosary, and over her were placed a black stole with white crosses and a long mantle.

The nuns, who were laboring in the forest on the river Satis picking berries, were sent home by Seraphim, who told them, "My joys, go quickly to Diveevo, where Maria, the great servant of God, has departed to our Lord!" He also sent the monks and townspeople of Sarov to the funeral, and instructed the civilian girls to dress well for the funeral, comb their hair, and kneel at her coffin.

As to the cause of her death, he said, "When the church was being built in Diveevo, everybody would carry two or three stones, but she would carry five or six at once while praying. And so, she strained her body."

While she was still alive, he used to tell one of her mill sisters, "Our Lord has twelve apostles, the Queen of Heaven has twelve maidens, and I have twelve of you. From among the twelve I have chosen Maria to be my bride in the hereafter, where she will be your Superior."

In winter, before the construction of the mill started, two of his favorite sisters from Diveevo came to Seraphim in Sarov. One of them was Maria. He took them to the remote hermitage, which was his first visit after his life there. On the way, he scooped up water in his glove from the healing spring and gave it to the sister who was sick with a cough. In the cell of the hermitage, the elder gave them each a lit candle and asked them to stand on either side of the cross: Maria on the right and the other on the left, and, standing between them, prayed for a long time. Then they kissed the cross. The rest of the day, they were cleaning the cellar, and in the evening they returned to Sarov. Beginning from that day Seraphim and his sisters began cutting down trees for the mill. A furnace was placed in the hermitage where the sisters could rest.

That prayer in the forest with the two sisters, one of whom he later made Sister Superior at the mill, and the other, Maria, Sister Superior over all of them in the other world, was undoubtedly of a very special significance.

The name Motovilov is also connected with Diveevo. Seraphim healed him in September of 1831. He was young but severely ill for three years, and his servants brought him to the nearby hermitage. He was completely weakened and crippled by rheumatism when entering Seraphim's cell but emerged from it healthy. All who were there saw it.

Notes of Motovilov's conversations with Seraphim have been preserved.

In November, after his healing, Motovilov came to the hermitage.

The elder seated him on a tree stump, and himself sat squatting in front of him. The ground was covered with snow, and snow was falling from above. The elder began telling him about the purpose of the Christian life, which consists of seeking and receiving the Holy Spirit of God. He explained to Motovilov what the Holy Spirit is, that it is the very breath of life, the immortal breath that makes man higher than other creatures and God-like. "Adam," said Seraphim, "was created without being subject to the forces of any of the elements created by God, that neither water could drown him, nor fire could burn him, nor earth could consume him in its chasms, nor air could harm him by any of its actions. He was admired by all as the perfect crown of creation. Adam gave to every creature such a name that fully represented all the qualities and all the attributes that was given to it by the grace of God." By the Spirit of God he could understand "the words of the Lord, and communications of the holy angels, the language of all the beasts, the birds, and of the creeping creatures that dwell upon the earth, and all that is now hidden from us, which to Adam was made manifest. However, Adam and Eve had prematurely eaten from the tree of knowledge, thus losing the gift that Christ would bring back to men. Yet the Spirit of God continued to work on earth unceasingly; for example, in the prophets, the sibyls, the Greek philosophers, without being revealed to men in its fullness. Christ restored the human prototype and opened the way for men to become again a vessel of the Spirit of God, when He breathed this Spirit into the twelve Apostles."

Seraphim spoke of the revelation of the Holy Spirit as an indescribable light.

It was getting late. The snow continued to fall. Motovilov wanted to know how a man can recognize the presence of the Holy Spirit in oneself.

"Both of us now, my dear," said Seraphim, "are filled with the Spirit of God! Why are you not looking at me?"

"I can't look at you, Father, for lightning bolts are coming from your eyes. Your face has become as bright as the sun, and my eyes ache with pain."

Seraphim said, "Fear not, God-loving soul! Now you yourself have become as bright as I am. Now you are in the fullness of the Spirit of God, otherwise you would not be able to see me like this."

And bending down to him, Seraphim asked Motovilov again, "Why, my dear, will you not look me in the eye? Look without fear, for the Lord is with us!"

When Motovilov looked at Seraphim's face this time, it was as if it was the center of the sun. Motovilov saw the movement of the starets' lips, heard his voice, felt that someone was holding him by the shoulders, but he saw neither these hands, nor himself, but only a blinding light that illuminated the snow-covered meadow and the snow falling from above.

Seraphim was asking him how he was feeling.

"I feel such silence and peace in my soul that I cannot express it in words."

The elder spoke to him about peace, the peace of which the Lord told his disciples, "My peace I give unto you; not as the world gives, I give it to you."

"What else do you feel?"

"An extraordinary bliss!"

And Seraphim explained to him the feeling of bliss.

"And what else?"

"An unusual joy in my heart, a sweet fragrance and much warmth in my body," Motovilov answered.

The elder spoke about the joy of a man born in the spirit. "When a woman gives birth, she has sorrow when her hour comes; but when she gives birth to a child, she does not remember sorrow because of the joy that a human being is born into the world. In the world you will have sorrow, but when you will see Me, your heart will rejoice, and no one will take your joy from you."

"How is it, my dear soul, that you feel warmth?" Seraphim asked with a smile. "We are sitting in the forest. It is wintertime, and there is snow under our feet and snow on both of us." He explained to Motovilov the source of the warmth and of the sweet fragrance that he felt.

At the end of the conversation the elder said to him, "Our faith consists not in the words of earthly wisdom, but in the manifestation of power and spirit. This is the state that we are in now," and he beseeched Motovilov to remember this hour.

Motovilov had many conversations with Seraphim, and Seraphim saw that there was sadness in his heart. It was because he loved a girl and longed for her. The girl was sixteen years old then.

"What are you saying, God-loving soul! No, no, your God-destined bride is now eight years and a couple of months old."

Motovilov was upset and did not understand him. Then the old man questioned him about another girl with whom he had previously had an affair. Motovilov was frightened, struck by Seraphim's insight. Learning that that girl was settled, the elder said, "I pray and beg you, God-loving soul, do not ignore my words and do not forget my humble request," said Seraphim, bowing to the ground. He stood up and continued, "If ever, somewhere, a maiden is being slandered on your account, and people say that she is an intimate friend of yours and that you live with her, then, even though you have not touched her at all, I beg you to respect the request of the humble Seraphim—to consecrate her to yourself."

"How do I consecrate her to me, father?"

"I do not speak of sanctification: as a pure virgin she is holy as she is. Consecrate her to be your companion; that is, take her as your wife, simply put, and marry her."

And he bowed down once more to the ground. Motovilov fell at the elder's feet and assured him that he had known no one since he had loved that girl, and especially since he had been visiting Seraphim.

But Seraphim continued bowing to him and asking on behalf of a girl who was like an angel both in spirit and in flesh, a peasant by birth.

Seraphim was speaking of a girl who was eight years old at the time. She was a niece of one of the Diveevo sisters and was being brought up in the monastery. Later Motovilov married her.

Motovilov called himself a servant of the Mother of God and of Seraphim. He was given a commandment by Seraphim to serve "the sisters of the mill." To him Seraphim revealed how he wrestled with the dark forces for a thousand days and a thousand nights. Once, the elder told him about the power of these forces in the world, from which only the grace of Christ can save mankind. "The slightest of them with its claw can turn the whole earth upside down," he said.

"But, father, do demons have claws?" doubted the learned nobleman.

"Oh, God-loving soul, God-loving soul, what do they teach you at your university? You know that demons have no claws. They can't be depicted by any human analogy, but analogy is necessary, so they depict them black, hideous and with claws."

In their last conversation, the elder said to Motovilov, "That is how it is, God-loving soul: if someone condemns you—bless them, if someone slanders you—accept it, if someone maligns you—rejoice! Such is our path!"

Motovilov devoted his life to honoring Seraphim's memory as best he could. His love for Seraphim and his religious devotion often manifested in a rather unusual manner, but his heart was true and selfless. Strange illnesses befell him, only to be cured by spiritual means. As years went by, the strangeness in him increased. He traveled tirelessly to holy places and was known everywhere as "the nobleman in the red coat." He walked around Diveevo with his head uncovered at all times in all seasons of the year.

Once a day he walked around the holy ditch along which, as Seraphim said, "the Heavenly Queen herself had walked." He crawled over the ice-covered ground on all fours. Pelageya Ivanovna, a Diveevo blessed fool, used to say to him with love, "You are a mad man, Nikolka! Just as mad as I am!"

In 1831 at the feast of Annunciation, Seraphim had a great vision. With him at the time was the Diveevo Eldress Evdokia. It was early in the morning. Seraphim placed his mantle over her and began to recite the Akathists. Then he said, "Do not be afraid, do not be discouraged... The Grace of God is coming to us."

Suddenly there arose a wind-like sound, the door swung open by itself, there appeared a shining light, a sweet fragrance wafted across the room, and they heard voices chanting.

Seraphim, falling on his knees, whispered, "Oh, blessed pure Virgin, Most Holy Mother of God!"

In came two angels holding branches abloom with spring flowers. They were followed by John the Baptist, John the Evangelist, the Most Holy Mother of God, and twelve maidens.

The conversation between Her and Seraphim was about Diveevo, and, blessing the elder, She said, "Soon, my beloved, you will be with Us."

The elder was growing weak. He was receiving fewer visitors. Upon parting, he would say, "We will see each other on the other side. It is better there, much better." And he awaited death as the greatest of all joys. On Sunday, January 1, 1833, after communion, Seraphim visited all the icons, kissing them, bade farewell to all the brethren, and felt greatly tired. On that day he came out of his cell three times to look at the place where he indicated earlier that he should be buried.

In the evening, father Paul, who lived in the next cell, heard Seraphim's quivering, old, but joyous voice singing Easter songs: "Christ's Resurrection has been seen...," "O glow, New Jerusalem...," "O Easter great and holy, most sacred Easter...."

At six o'clock in the morning, father Paul smelled smoke in the hall. He knocked on Seraphim's door. There was no answer. Afraid of a fire, father Paul called the monks who were on their way to Matins. The dawn was just beginning to break.

In the near darkness, the door in the smoke-filled hall was broken open. The canvases and books were smoldering. Snow was used to put out the fire. A candle was brought in. The elder was kneeling before the icon of the Mother of God, which he always called "the Joy of all Joys." His hands were folded in a cross on his chest, his head was lowered. They wanted to wake him up. But he had moved on.

That was a brief summary of Saint Seraphim's life. But he is more than what can be said about him by recounting his deeds and quoting his words.

His words and his deeds belong to time. They are only a mere shadow of what was accomplished in the spirit, of what is timeless. A word, however true it may be, when repeated by other voices in a different time, can become a lie. Similarly a deed, not taken in connection with an entire life, is an empty and dead thing. Frequently such words or deeds, when recounted, may become a wall between us and a living spirit that lived in a different time and spoke and acted in a manner characteristic of its time.

One must be able not to stop at the form, but to look beyond it, towards the spirit which the form served and which is alive, which, being true to its own nature, would speak differently today than it did yesterday. But too often people are inclined to anchor everything and to fasten what is alive with nails. When the essential is removed from a symbol, there arises idolatry and one begins to worship the form, the shadow, the likeness, not the spirit. In Sarov I was surprised by this attitude in those who were called to keep the legacy of the elder alive, to pass on his truly human example. There I saw an outward worship of things and forms which was a betrayal of the elder's spirit, who intentionally clothed the sublime in a childlike, humble, and often odd form in order to keep this form gentle, flowing, and transparent, so that its shadow would not block reality. After all, the humble Seraphim had replaced the reason of this world with wisdom, which was foolishness in men's eyes. For it was appearances that he wanted to break, giving them only the value of a symbol.

"Similarity is necessary," Seraphim would say, so the burning candles in his cell, and the dried bread which he handed out, and the stakes, and the mill with twelve maidens—all of these are analogies of the loftiest spiritual reality, all are sacraments, for he remained quiet about the most sublime, but out of his love he strengthened and consoled all who came to him.

This became clear to me in Sarov.

It was time for the All-Night Vigil. As the sun was setting, people came to the gates under the monastery's white bell tower. Thousands came; elderly men, their heads as white as snow, and young, bearded men, with hair as black as coal. They all had dark, sunburned faces. From beneath their thick eyebrows, their luminous, wise eyes brightly shone. There were many young and many very old women too.

They were humble, burdened yet filled with faith. I saw much suffering and pain combined with meekness and a look of resignation in almost all of them. They kept streaming and streaming towards the temple under the bell tower. Seeing those resigned eyes that, when looking at their surroundings, see something else, I realized what Seraphim meant to these people. For them he is not to be found here, just like his Russia, is not yet here. For this people are not fully present here, not on the earth, laboring, covered in sweat, over the earth, praying for the earth, longing for the earth, but not bound by it, and not accepting the earth that is too heavy in its present form, trampled on by Judas.

And when on the next day the coffin of St. Seraphim was carried round the church, and thousands of colorful linen ribbons, forming bridges in the air over the crowd, flew towards the coffin, I imagined the hands that sowed and pulled flax all over Russia, the hands that spun and wove it in dark huts all over Russia, the eyes that held no hope in a tear-filled woman's lot—at that moment I understood what Seraphim was for all of Russia.

On the way to the hermitage, I saw many people who were sick and crippled. They were sitting on

Seraphim's rock and also by the spring. Some of them had transparent, suffering eyes, and I realized that it was not the teaching, not the words that Seraphim gave to this people, but his power, a mighty power that, judging by his gaze, could have burned the land like a firestorm, but instead it was kindled by such love, which will not pass away when all prophecies pass away. It poured over the earth, poured on the spring and stones and grasses, imbuing them with a healing mercy. Seraphim implored the water, the stone and the trees to restore the people; and his embrace can still be felt in the flowing waters of the spring and in the fertile earth all around it.

We can even say that the rock symbolically represents Seraphim's loving heart and the spring waters flow from Seraphim's heart.

Saint Seraphim's spirit stewards over Russia, and the earth and its waters are faithful to it.

Yet people have forgotten. I looked at the monastery in Sarov and Diveevo, at peddling, prying and idolatry, and I asked myself, "Where is the Diveevo that according to the words of Saint Seraphim will be the spiritual stronghold of Russia? Where is Seraphim's prophecy?"

In Diveevo, near the old Kazan Church, three graves lie under a tree. In the middle grave rests the founder of Diveevo, Mother Alexandra Melgunova, on her right lies Elena Vasilievna, and on her left, Maria.

Here is that temple in which the elder much delighted, the divine temple above Diveevo. I wondered if Seraphim saw it in the souls of Elena and Maria? Those souls, torn away from the earth too early, their great energies plucked up prematurely and given to the higher powers to fight evil on earth, they are like golden swords in the hands of the angels, and this is where Russia's stronghold is.

Little Maria, who tied her shawl so that she could not see anything else but the road to Sarov and the tips of her feet, who carried in her heart Seraphim's image and the truth of his revelations, who was Seraphim's Spirit Bride, will she not stand by his side as a guardian over the future Russia?

What do we really know about the treasures of those souls whom Seraphim gathered in Diveevo—the souls of the hot-tempered and misfortunate Manturov, of the foolish and unreasonable Motovilov, of the common, barely literate mill maidens, or of the holy fools of Diveevo? Seraphim knew their strength and foresaw the future.

Russia remains silent. Her spirit has not yet descended into her body. It hovers above her, it is greater than her. Because all that is here on earth is only a mere shadow of something else. Only a symbol, a likeness. Just such a symbol is the "ditch," which will rise up to the heavens at the time of the Antichrist, and Seraphim's "dried bread," and his mill with the twelve maidens.

He who begins to understand the language of things, for whom things are signs through which spiritual essences are revealed, will understand this likeness.

The mystery of the grain is revealed to the one whose soul, cleansed of passions, is ready to receive the spirit.

Such a soul sees the invisible through all that is visible. All the elements, all of nature become for it a living language of the spirit. Such a person can embrace in the symbol of "dried bread" the mystery of the Mother Earth, who was united with the sun, the Christ mystery.

It is remarkable that in ancient legends, where the truths of the spiritual world are clothed in images, we find tales about windmills with maidens tending them. By actualizing this windmill on earth, Seraphim performed a sacrament for the whole of Russia.

In the sacramental language of Christianity, the soul that has passed through spiritual purification and is ready to receive into itself the world Spirit was always called a Virgin pure and wise. The epitome of this pure Wisdom on earth was the Mother of God.

In the bond between Seraphim and the Virgin Mary lies the mystery of all of Russia. Is not Russia a soul, waiting "to receive the Holy Spirit of God," which, illuminating her in all her uniqueness, and purifying her passionate fire, will sanctify her for eternity in the divine Wisdom of Sophia?

From the thicket of the remote pine forest of Sarov, through the blue eyes of the humble Seraphim, the soul of Russia continues to shine, waiting for the future.

About the author

Margarita Vasilievna Woloschin (*née* Sabashnikova) was born in Moscow and traveled extensively with her family already as a child, in Europe and throughout Russia. In her youth, she was recognized as a painter of great promise, and was well known as an artist by the age of twenty-one.

Her active, searching spirit and deeply religious nature led her, in 1905, to Rudolf Steiner, who was then the leader of the German Section of the Theosophical Society. This encounter proved decisive for her entire life. She united herself with the work of Rudolf Steiner, heard many of his early lecture cycles, and became a friend and coworker of those who first carried forward the impulse of anthroposophy. She worked as a painter, under Rudolf Steiner's direction, on the original Goetheanum in Dornach, Switzerland.

Her love of Russia and her wish to be part of its destiny drew her back to Petersburg and Moscow during the early days of the revolution. Thus, between 1917 and 1922 Woloschin was an active leader of the Russian Anthroposophical Society and was the first to bring the art of eurythmy to Russia.

At the end of 1922, seeing no possibility for free cultural life in Soviet Russia, Woloschin left for Germany. The Russian Anthroposophical Society soon ceased to exist.

She lived the rest of her life in Stuttgart, wholly dedicated to anthroposophy until the end.

Her memoir, *Die grüne Schlange* (*The Green Snake*), was published in German in 1954; it contains priceless material about the construction of the First Goetheanum and the early days of the anthroposophical movement.

Margarita Woloschin died on November 2, 1973, aged 91.